Build on a Dream

Another Collection of Thoughts in Verse

Arunav Barua

Order this book online at www.trafford.com
or email orders@trafford.com

Most Trafford titles are also available at major online book retailers.

Printed in the United States of America.

ISBN: 978-1-4907-4852-8 (sc)
ISBN: 978-1-4907-4851-1 (e)

Trafford rev. 11/20/2014

North America & international
toll-free: 1 888 232 4444 (USA & Canada)
fax: 812 355 4082

To,

LONDA (Chiranjib Barua);

Brother…you spoke with your silence and left a void
in all our lives…

AND…

As usual, to you—Duffer!

FOREWORD:

Arunav Barua rhymes with reason, and sometimes with passion too. His verse has the innocence of country songs and sometimes even the ease of the Blues. He addresses a whole range of concerns, from routine human realities to larger problems of mankind. It is when he takes leave from the sentiments that he avows and advocates, however laudable they are, that he strikes the authentically immediate and his idiom also takes on a personal intensity, as in the following:

> Soaring like a bird in flight
> Almost touching that untamed blue,
> Illusion lasts, but for seconds
> Back again to that solitary nest,
> Tomorrow is another flight.
> Tomorrow is another dream
> Tomorrow is…
> Thankful it is…

The privacy of a diary entry is feelingly recaptured in 'The Diary' where earthy concerns do not quarrel with emotional reaching out:

> Pages of mirth, pages of laughter
> Black binding, leather, like lost tears…
> I read you again from end to end;
> The news is that the rains are foretold
> All else is history…
> Let me get my umbrella........

Over and above significant pieces like 'The Colour of Laughter', it is the close encounters of the first kind that I find more reassuring as in the first poem of the collection, 'A Dialogue and an Escape'.

Arunav has a bright future and I wish him 'God Speed'.

Pradip Acharya,
Former Professor of English,
Cotton College,
Guwahati, Assam.

A DIALOGUE AND AN ESCAPE

I was alone today, walking nowhere in time,
If thoughts had value, could give one for a dime.
A sudden gust of wind introduced me to pain,
Ah! Welcome, as the dry Earth welcoming rain...
I looked around searching for a release,
Can I forget 'me' for a while; a few moments, please?
Wherever I go, even in the land of 'nod',
I tag 'me' along through all the paths I've ever trod!

Then I chance upon a table and a few chairs,
Laid out in that forest, a secret lair,
I sit on a chair, willing to play out this game
I wait for someone, though feel the excuses lame!
You arrive in time, right out of thin air
I manage two words, I say, "Hey there!"
Then we have a conversation of catch up true
I forget 'me' for a while, I do!

Dialogue it is; an escape from the eternal 'me'...

(13th of January 2014)

A FULL CIRCLE

It has been long now, it has,
 Since that evening, you and me...
Sadly, time never does last,
 Are you happy now, that smile can I see?
I am still me, some changes here and there
I remember I loved looking at you and would often stare!

There were moments then, I often remember,
 Moments of sheer joy spent with you
I went back today to that cold day in December,
 That blanket on us and our love so true!
Perchance we meet again, can we please?
Time marches on and mere wishes these...

I would look at you and tell you so much,
 How I counted days and their sad nights...
How lonely I felt without your soft touch!
 Would morrow dawn upon us a morning bright?
Time never stops even in momentous joy,
 Your snap in hand and all I can do is try...

Time has come full circle...

(August 2013)

A MAN'S NATURE

Grow towards that sky in careless abandon
Does it give you that desire for freedom?
In a trees' nature is, but to grow
As a boatman's is to row!

The scent of his prey in the forest,
Even if they be wee birds in their nest
In a tiger's nature is, but to hunt
Can the boatman fly? Well, he can't!

Hearing the tweet, that musical voice
Does it not stop you from rolling dice?
In a bird's nature is but to chirp,
A nest where she can play her harp.

Each his own, a different species,
Every man, the world differently sees
In a man's nature is but to be different
No two the same, try but they can't!

Such is the story that survives
Some men heal, some kill with knives!

(July 2014)

A MIDSUMMER NIGHT"'S DREAM

Apollo lays out the path in order,
The conceited believe it's a walk like any other
Their ego stops them mid-stream
Walking awake and yet feel it's a dream!
The walk brings out the best in Mr. Tweety
Maybe because he does so with humility…

Those birds chirp their joy as they walk,
Am sure like Dolphins, they have their talk!
A castle there, on that Horizon
A princess on that tower waiting for her prince to come
I, Tweety, walk on and reach the castle
I see her with eyes bedazzled!

I start my climb, step by step, stone to stone
Reaching her window, I see she is all alone
She gives me her hands and I kiss her palms
I look at her as love begging for alms
Alas! She picks up a bottle of port, hits me, and my eyes go dim
I awake and see it had all been A Midsummer Night's dream!

(June 22, 2014)

A MUSICAL INTERLUDE

A starry night helps the mind wander,
That sad tune accompanies the silent evening
The stars promise new worlds
Is music also a truth there?
For, it does seem silly,
Now that I think about it
Music has to be a truth everywhere!

That rhythm that beat on the drums of yore
Find expression in tales and lore
The masters had so much to say,
They said it then, and today,
Yes, new worlds are easily thought up,
But then, this question is always brought up
Is music also a truth there?

All the sights of all the worlds
Is but a dream unfurled
Well, wish there is music in them!

(September 3, 2014)

A THOUGHT AND ITS ACTION

A doorway between thought and action;
Work never does go out of fashion!
I think of a tree; but is it enough?
Unless a seed is planted, seeing one is tough!
Even the rains need clouds to rain
Even sorrow needs tears for the pain…

Having love in our heart, love absolute,
Without that kiss and hug, it is just a prelude
Smiles now; even laughter needs effort,
That caring touch, that shoulder of support
We all have thoughts, grand and ideal,
Change it to action; let's make a deal!

Pleasure, or pain, or just a cup of tea
Nature is the teacher; we just have to see
Learn from her, in her we dwell,
Every action from thought, an unuttered spell!
We have a journey; a path our own
Alas! only the direction may be shown!

Let us go back and convert every thought into action
Let us build a world which rests on perfection…

(8th of January 2014)

A TRYST WITH ETERNITY

Every life has that; it is surely felt
That tryst with eternity, the first glance
Sadness shows it, sometimes in joy held,
As it forms a shape beyond mere chance.

Instances when we do behold
Moments that pierce the veil
Seeing through and yet we hold,
Footsteps marking the path, the trail!

A knock on the door, and the arrival,
Ah! Welcome to my world again
I kept searching for you moment, if you shall
Is this tryst the same with all men?

Eternity is not too long a word…
Yet, when felt, the longest ever heard.

(May 4th 2014)

A VIRTUE NOT EASILY ASSIGNED

Innocence, a virtue not easily assigned,
    Either you have it or not,
Its all in the mind…
    That passing moment, that stray thought,
The heart answers its call,
Somewhere, we do find it in all!

A lake, a few meditating birds,
    Caught in a cage by themselves wrought
A cacophony of cries begins to be heard,
    In the end, it all comes down to naught.
Show me then how your eyes endure,
How, even in a shell, they reflect the pure.

Thinking without thought seems like the norm,
    Feelings not understood with ease,
Having shape but not any definite form…
    Give me that smile of innocence please
I hate it when you cry, let me gently tease!
From all that is unsaid, let me now cease…

Time now to wake up and in innocence bathe…

(Mid August 2013)

AFTERNOON

As I sit in a restless stupor,
The world just goes by in a haze
The best dreams seldom find life
A life which is, but of memories past
I try and live again, still waiting,
I dream on, hoping it translates
Into a reality known, that can be touched
Are afternoons always this morose?

A step or two towards that reality
Finding my self first and then the rest
You show me things in sleep
Which somehow don't find their answers
Breaking away from the herd
Away from everything I know as sure,
Ah! But these are just afternoon thoughts,
Are afternoons always this morose?

(27th of April 2014)

ANSWERS

A deafening silence felt in the vicinity,
Of time, counted in the shadows of this city
I walk the streets knowing no face,
Memories, hurt, anger, hoping to erase
Them, and their unsure smiles
I keep walking, and slowly forget the miles!

History is written over every stone,
Uncovering memories is a hard task alone
Comfort in the known, fear of the unknown,
A glimpse of sure history shown
I now bid adieu to all I once knew,
I search for answers in the fresh morning dew!

There, I had smiled!
There, I had wept!
There, I had been me!

(September 8, 2014)

BEING

If my being is a question for me,
Kindly explain how I should look and see...
That patch of Sunlight and clouds amidst the blue,
Wish I could see myself with eyesight new.
'Being is to be', certainly is the definition,
Why then can't I see; no answer, no reason,
Is my being defined by my thought?
With consciousness then, this battle being fought!

A questing mind, even being, just a phase,
The choices we make define our consciousness,
I see me here without you, a state!
Yet I choose to smile, a choice I make...
Do I have that, can we make that choice?
Even in sorrow, give joy a voice;
I feel we will find it then
Our being very close to 'heaven'!

(Sept 2013)

BREATHE

Somewhere between then and now
Stars have changed but little…
Summer is almost always the same
Winter is as cold as always…
Me?
Well, they say experience does things to you
They say with time comes wisdom
Rich in experience, the heart aches though
For those lost in the labyrinth of time
Hope says we all get back together,
When every moment wishes reliving
Every laugh
Every tear
Every moon seen together
'Lost' is a word that would define me,
Yet, I hold on to the Earth
Even as I look at that star,
I try, and…
Breathe

(28th of May 2014)

BUILD ON A DREAM

Build on a dream, if you can,
Set it aflame and onward you send
A little brick here, some there,
Onward, and yet, is it even fair?
Someday, someone would live
In your dream…
Make it home…
Give their hearts…
Someday, someone would grow up there,
Have a childhood laid bare
Bricks and stones…
Bricks and stones…
Do they make up that dream?
Your toil…
Your dream…
Now you see it fulfilled
Now your dream
Gives dreams to others
In the end it was all…
Building on a dream!

(21/11/13)

CLOSE YOUR EYES AND SEE

Close your eyes and see
The unseen, in me
Open your heart and feel,
That feeling which makes you kneel.
I talk of times past;
When we believed forever we'd last.

There was a passage of time then,
Seeing without sight was easy when…
Now it's all in the old trunk,
Where all our memories we debunk.
Should we open that trunk and find
That sweet passage of time, oh! So kind?

If it was possible, we'd relive each day,
Travel back in time and have our say.
Journey, a journey undertaken as well
To travel in that passage where forever we dwell,
I tell you again to close your eyes and see,
Feel what your heart says; the unseen in me!

(Oct end 2013)

COMMON GROUND

It has been a long voyage,
All of mankind, a silent rage
Built up through time, in the present,
Wishes, hopes, dreams, love; all sent
To a place unknown, somewhere in time,
The bells in my mind ring, a silent chime.

There is the seen and the unseen
As we form our hopes, our team!
Let us travel through time, to the now,
Don't ask me, but tell me how...
We would ask questions, unheard, unsought,
One as a whole, one team, one thought.

Man, he has arrived in the present,
His feelings, his thoughts, to heaven, lent.
All as one, let us seek the answer,
Does she know, or is it futile to ask her?
Come to a common ground then
Collective consciousness; let us our thoughts send!

(11th of October 2013)

CONVERSATION WITHOUT END

Surely trees talk!
Not mere syllables...
Not words either...
They talk in flowers
They converse in fruits
Every time I eat that pear,
It's the tree...
It is telling me it loves me!
Every nest the bird builds,
Is the tree, giving shelter

The flowers are a different tongue
They are poems;
The rose is a beautiful sonnet...
All verse, all beautiful...
An expression of love
The kind seen in fairy tales
The bees their kith and kin
Their messengers...
Spreading the love
Surely trees talk!

The conversation is getting interesting now
As I watch nature in her glory
Talk to me!

(September 2014)

DIVINE MESSAGES

Far, yet near; my eyes could see
The leaves on that yonder tree
A setting Sun, tinges of red
Melancholy, a feeling unlike any
Those leaves, they wave!
A message in a bottle, without the bottle!
Lost at sea, wish I could be,
Those leaves, they speak!

Now, I give it time to ripen
The Sun, it will set and my message,
My message, I will lose
Those leaves, they see!
They wave at me, I lend my ears,
I wave back with my eyes
I sing a song and hope that:
Those leaves, they hear!

(5th of May 2014)

DONE LIVING

Done Living
Pain plenty
Joy fleeting
Name: life!
Sorrow: tears
Happiness: laughter
Meaning?
Search awaited
Answers sought
Questions myriad
Can this be life?
Done living…

Hope in fingers crossed
Farewell noise
Farewell chaos
Welcome order
Welcome feelings
Welcome love
Fingers still crossed
Hope: ah!
Hope: oh!
Sunrise…
Sunset…
Done living

By the clock.

(4th of July 2013)

DUTY AND DUST

Lying on the plain ground;
    Some particles of dust, I found,
Interpreting what they were meant to say
    'Dust to dust', benign, the particles lay!
Tell me your story dust particle…
    Was I formed from you, a gentle trickle?

I let the dust fall from my hand,
    Their story remains a secret of the land!
Its time to put back leisure,
    In her box; a secret treasure!
Duty beckons, time of being busy,
    Ah! Nostalgia now, those moments lazy…

I dream of you, dust and time,
    If beginning finds its end, all would be fine
Let me take you up again in my hand
    Dust, tell me the tales of this land!
Now its time, duty beckons again,
    I will keep your secret intact, even in rain!

See the flowers blooming, is it spring?
Duty? Lets do ours, and then the dust song sing!

30/07/2013

FACTS REMAIN

Facts remain...
Of a journey enacted from birth,
A narrow domain...
Within reach of this, the Earth!
Learning and mistakes together,
Mould the human form forever...

Facts remain...
Of a questing mind seeking answers,
An unending chain...
As an unformed mind carefully nursed,
The winds hold as much mystery
As all books and their history!

Facts remain...
of the pinnacle of the human condition
As tears hide pain...
remnants found in every nation,
Truth, the search we are all engrossed in,
Hard to find in this loud din!

Facts remain...

(September 14, 2014)

FATHOM THE LOVE

Evening again, pen in hand,
Fantasies and dreams meet,
In the gallery of thoughts
The company of feelings
Do not suffice in this lonesome heart
If love could be measured
Could it be, even of potential?
So much to give, so much to share...
Fathom the love!

Been long now, yet everyday feels new,
You are a word, a name I have not met yet,
Not met; yet I hope and yet I search
For that meeting etched in dreams,
Someday, somewhere, we will...
My eyes will catch yours and know at once,
That we were meant to be,
All of eternity would await that second...
Fathom the love!

(14th February, 2014)

FEEL

Gave birth to desire
The heart knowing not...
Where that lock was lost,
The key in eternity
Desire...
Desire?
An acceptance of the myth
Fact turning into the
Unreal
Yet there
Yet known
Yes! All I can say now
Is that it was long,
That wait...
Ah! To be able to look
To see without judgement
To feel without remorse
Freedom...
Freedom?
Walls created by yourself
They hold you for
Eternity...
Welcome then,
Lets unfeel the felt!

(June 2014)

GIVING AWAY HOPE

Not I, but my thoughts,
They create in me a will of sorts
A silent, unnamed desire
I see an angel sleeping in her lair.
She opens her eyes and calls out,
Surprised, I call back, I almost shout!

We have a conversation of smiles
Am I happy, or am I just feeling high?
She smiles again and says out loud;
"Here, take this...its hope without doubt."
I thank her and carry hope in my heart
With hope now my thoughts silently flirt.

Hope bountiful I now possess
If I give it away, will it be my loss?
I decide to test this thought O' mine,
I give away hope as I would give time
Those in need, now I saw smile,
Hope can be given in such sweet design.

Here! Would you like some hope?
Take this, give it away and elope!

(2nd of December 2013)

I SEE YOU AS I SEE ME

Evening sways into night; slowly, imperceptibly,
Lights around, and one, just above me
Night and day, darkness and light together
Thoughts refuse to do their bidding; wait for later,
This passage of being is, but a narrow domain
Stars shine down, their memories are all that remain!

I see myself when I go to that almirah
Howdy!... is what I say to the mirror
I wait for the reply and see him/me smile
My thoughts take on a new turn, I leave with a sigh!
All this happening as day turns to night
Feeling is true, well more than seeing without sight!

(1st of May 2014)

I TAKE UP MY PEN

Back again to that open window,
A year's journey spent in lying low;
What is a year, but a moment's notice?
Yes, a pleasant show, a pleasant show, this!

Come then, I tell my raging heart,
This is, but just another start!
I can still sing, you know
Find myself in that mirror, show...

That tree is the same as I had left,
Did it miss me when I was bereft?
Now, I find myself again in word
Lost, yet a part of that human herd!

I know I have to find my rhythm again
I smile! For now, I take up my pen...

(July 5th 2014)

IMAGINATION

There is a land unknown,
Breaking beyond chains of the known
The chains were strong,
Held the Earth through wrong...
The known is, but a narrow domain
To travel beyond, yes, there is a lane,
We have thought up a word for that nation,
In passing, we just call it imagination!

The known holds me down on Earth,
The unknown shows me possible rebirth
I prefer imagination any day,
Though I travel beyond reality, if I may!
Creating worlds beyond sadness and joy,
With new worlds my heart does toy
Now, this battle fought in my mind,
True, the mind is, at last I find!

(September 5, 2014)

IS HAPPINESS A CRIME?

A man with a secret;
	He keeps it safe from thunder
His destiny, he hopes to get,
	He guards it from greedy plunder.
Distance and space carry no meaning
Some day, a sad song he'll sing!

Ah! Out with it now,
	His secret is his being
He knows, he understands, and how!
	Blind to destiny, yet seeing…
A knowledge unlike all men,
Someone has termed it, 'Dasein'!

A conscious mind, a seeking heart,
Safe from the wild ways of this world,
Safe from the fallacies of this Earth
To seek, to find, to search and to mould…
Now its time, he wakes up again,
Is happiness a crime; is all he asks then.

(October 27, 2013)

IS IT ME?

As the droplets attack the windowpanes
Vision blurs; the outside becomes chaos
The colours, they stand nonetheless
A world of only colour seen in the blur,
The colours, they suit my melancholy mood
Is it me? Yes, I am a little upset today...

Thought precedes action, they say; the wise
With me, its action which precedes thought
Then the burden of conflicting judgement
Taking apart that action and questioning why...
The rains are welcome, they suit my mood
Is it me? Yes, I am a little upset today...

A feather born free flying against the windowpane,
It sticks like a thought you cant forget,
The winds, they blow with great strength,
Gathering everything meant to be a loss
Let me search the winds for that elusive answer
Is it me? Yes, I am a little upset today...

(June 21, 2014)

IT RAINED TODAY

It rained today, my heart felt it,
The skies though were a clear blue
The Sun looking and shining through
Your eyes, and what that smile did to them
I would give a kingdom to look again,
See I don't have one, so I will just give my life…

You were as close to an angel as I had ever seen,
If fate had decided otherwise so much could have been…
Ah! Life though, is not like the movies
Happy endings are felt, but in dreams
I see you there, standing all alone,
Just as I was, as alone as you…

It was fate that took the next steps,
All I did was looked at you,
Years later when everything is gone
Feelings remain of a love that was strong,
Yes, it rained today, after an eon,
My heart felt it, my eyes the clouds…

(May, 2014)

KNIGHTS AND DAYS (Satire)

A brave one, that he was!
Attack without warning, making his enemy shudder,
His first blow was always lethal,
His fame slowly travelled beyond borders known
Did I tell you how he attacked a whole platoon?
Singlehandedly murdered that brave platoon of mosquitoes!
And then, the brave battle with the wild ones,
It does not make it any less that they were wild rats!
He even won a trophy for fifty laps
On his skipping rope...
Such was our brave knight, one of a kind...

Then, as fate would have it, he fell in love!
With a lady beauteous beyond measure
She reminded you of roses in spring,
Sometimes she reminded you of being shy...
Now, don't ask me why!
She was his lady fair and then some more.
Love changed him, made him soft,
We don't know how Cupid did that
All we know was that our knight was a brave cat!

(2nd of February 2014)

LAKE DISTRICT

I leave you behind…
    Too short an affair to call it love
Memory though, tells tales of its own kind,
    Forgetting you is going to be tough.
That passage of time writ large in my mind
Those hillocks, a valley, secrets, I find…

Coming back to the present…
    Your image writ large in memory,
That lake, in memory a dent,
    Will I ever lose your image unless I hurry?
That song I sang on that hill of yore
I sang on, sang till I was sore…

That cottage on the hillock,
    A room with Sunlight permeating,
A room of empty talk,
    Where the Laureate wrote his nature greeting
Poems of love, yes, romance!
Poems that render you into a trance…

The lakes were vast,
    Almost a sea…
A paradise you can almost trust!
    There, ah! How I remember me,
You left your mark, touched me true,
The word that defines me now is always 'blue'…

(Sept 2013)

LET LOVE BE...

Put a price on everything,
Let all be bought and sold...
This land of ours is old
And witness to an old art of
    Healing.

It's the heart that heals,
Buying and selling now
Has surpassed time, and how!
Need healing?
Buy a soul...
Need a friend?
Buy gifts...
Need seclusion?
Buy an island...
Need religion?
Buy faith...

It's a plea, a silent appeal,
To leave out one thing
From this continuous seal,
From the sly out of buying and selling
So that with true eyes we can see,

Please, let love be...

(12th of December 2013)

LOST IN TRANSLATION

I had a dream, one I saw everyday,
Green was the colour, golden the hue.
Hills and beauty writ large...
A walk was all it took to reach the gates
Which opened and closed of their own will
A climb on that hill, a rainbow...
A pot of gold and goodwill aplenty!
People I knew, some gone forever...
Yet, in my dream, there they were again.
Talk of times past, a silent Hooray!
Weeping, I questioned them where they went,
Why they had to go leaving me alone.
In my dream, they answered in riddles
Talk, but making no sense, some strange puzzle.
That dream didn't end there though...
Even the gold didn't matter
Reunion was such joy!
Earth we left behind and glad we did
For we met, all who had parted,
We walk together now,
In that land of my dreams
Once parted, now together,
Green was the colour, Golden the hue...

(Late August 2013)

MEMORY OF LOSS

Years ago we met, and felt,
Love arose, and, in that we dwelt,
Feelings such that in our heart
Time took on a meaning without thought!

A passage then of such joyous today's,
Travelling in time through love's maze.
Your eyes meant all, and, in your face
I saw reflected those carefree days!

Every meeting was gilded gold
Together, I dreamt, we'd grow old,
The first clouds were ominous
Then the dark rains hit us!

You had to leave, go your way,
I tried to go mine, kept feelings at bay...
Now it's gone, now it's over, yet I feel
A loss which even words can't seal!

(September 29, 2013)

NOW

Freedom at will,
A search...
For release from the constant
Me...
Will you hold and take me there?
My hand...
Ever ready to grasp, the truth,
I seek...
Days spent in futile reminisces
Their nights...
They whisper the word alone.

A full day, starting with
A full morn...
And ending never too soon with
A contented night...
Smiling beyond words to see
The quintessential me...
There in this passage, the end arrives,
Now...

(14th of October 2013)

ONLY SO FAR

A Statistician with his mean
A Doctor, his medicine…
Earth, with her motley crew,
All travelling towards redemption.
Lovers of wisdom
Still have a few books unread,
Trees attempt at growing taller
Science still has some marvels
Up her sleeve…
Space unexplored!
Galaxies not discovered!
Algebra to fit dimensions!
Time travel?

The 'Big Bang' did you say?
I heard a shot in the air!
Was that God shooting?
Adventures still await…
Gates left unopened
Close them to the world!
Lest some stranger should enter
Those gates…
And your heart…
I try and put words on paper,
I try to draw you out
Please keep in mind
I can only go so far and no further…

(28th of January 2014)

OUR DESTINY

As a precept to living,
All of knowledge is within us
A point so small, yet existing
All the known and unknown, the universe
Everything we can put a finger on
And some we can't, in a secret manner done.

A child can teach the art of existence
So much better than the knowledgeable,
A look at that flower, hope it's not just a glance
Am I saying experience spoils us? Or, is it a fable?
Come then, let us go back to that first kiss
Ah! You are smiling now; I will put that on my list!

As the knowledge of the flower in the seed,
As the knowledge of the child in the father,
The knowledge of the universe within us indeed!
Unflowering the secret, lets leave that for later
Lets join hands and embark on our journey,
Lest we are unjoined by cruel destiny!

(20/12/2013)

RA

Some joy this...
 That I see you now in shackles,
Whither that childhood mirth
 Those wondrous days of yore?
Let us search the morning for answers...

The Sun. the Sun, its all in the Sun
 I feel the freshness of the mornings
The unbridled happiness of now
 In the face of a new beginning,
Childhood, and that afternoon yet to come.

Midday, the heat gets to me
And I reflect back on morning
The beautiful moments past,
I toil and strive, break out in sweat
Age, and the evening awaited...

As a beautiful day slowly comes
To a much awaited end—
The morning's answers,
The afternoon's hard work,
All culminate in a beautiful orange sunset
Ra, lead me into the night...

(15/11/2007)

REMNANTS OF SUMMER

An autumn such; it lets not go,
Of the Summer Sun, wanting even more
The heat, the heat, this monstrosity!
Ah! Welcome rain; though you flood our city…

Until winter's cold forces you away,
Heat and cold, a battle being fought everyday.
Thou art not Summer, Autumn,
Leave this facade; come back to your rhythm.

I sense a chill in the air,
Someone is happy, somewhere…
Let us bid adieu to the heat,
Some relief this, comfort, we meet!

(5th of Oct 2013)

SECRETS OF THE EARTH

Every time I look at you
I stand up and notice something anew.
A moonlit night; your colour but silver,
Telling me things that mark you; clever!
I smile in this world created by your form,
Looking foolish, yet, this the norm
Believing in absurd destiny;
Wake and sleep; your image in me!

It would surprise many, the truth,
Your colour green, the eyes doth it soothe,
Did I just say Green now?
A Green love; possible, but how?
Then I have to go back
Thoughts of the present, from my mind, sack.
You were but a seed once,
Your branches, now, how they dance.

Yes! You are, you are a tree,
Outside my window, ah! My glee...

(20th of Oct 2013)

SEED

Release...
From the sea of ease
Stranger...
At every turn lies danger
Indecision...
Still walking with precision
Homecoming...
Giving rest to my heart's longing
A Nest...
Ah! Finally some rest
Question...
From my lonely bastion
Hunger...
Now, all that remains is anger
Fear...
Ah! All the chaos I hear
Order...
From now to eternity, a dream another
Evening...
A tired Sun slowly setting
Above...
I see the stars of light and love
Sleep...
At last, a dream of the sea deep
You...
Are all that remains which I know as true

(6th of March 2014)

SHADE TO THE SUN

When the going is a journey of tedium,
When every step taken is a toil in the Sun
Rest assured that rest will arrive
Somewhere, where a part of me is still alive
I draw a line definite and true,
Almost smiling away my blues…

The Sun, the toil, ah! need some shade

I had planted a tree in my childhood,
I figure I will sit beneath its shade, well, I should!
Come then, tree of my life…
Make me feel that I am still alive,
Let me go; shade to the Sun,
Am sure I am not the only one!

Life is, Sun to the shade, Shade to the Sun…

(14th of June 2014)

SHADOW GAMES

Trying hard, hand over heart
Is it even possible to define a shadow?
Yes it is, but then, is it?
The pages move of their own accord
That constant companion, but never there!
Yes, it is,
No, is not…

One thing is true though
Without light, there is no you,
Shadow…
Tried defining you today
Tried drawing your outline
Changing with time,
Yet, always the same!

Yes, the dark merges you
With an essence I would call mine
Light binds you to me
Thought of a name for you,
Unthought it in the night
Who needs names?
Well, shadows don't!

Then, realization strikes me…
Shadow, thou art the world!

SHOULD I GIVE IN?

The night had decided the plot
That fire burning within and without
Anger too, and sorrow; all thought!
The essence of being loses the bout
Should I give in, should I sacrifice?
Is life a gamble, a roll of dice?

Inherent in me is a well of desire
Sorrow too, shows its face sometimes
Anger and lies burn in their own pyre
Through it all, common hope shines
There, I said it! Do what you will
This gap between word and thought, fill!

Waiting, waiting for the bright morn to shine
Will you hold my hand, tell me you are mine?

(July 2014)

SOLACE IN DESPERATION

Been walking long now,
It's been a while, yes,
The miles just eat up the days
Where did the destination disappear?
A mad rush, everyone running,
Stranded here, in the middle of nowhere
I seek solace in desperation
Keep walking, they say; and I do.

The good news is tomorrow
Sadly, today is a race,
One we run everyday, today.
Some have stopped, given up,
It takes heart to understand
That we don't decide the track
That it's in the journey and not the destination
And yes, I seek solace in desperation.

(28th of Oct, 2013)

SPACE—TIME

I am here now…
That was then, not any more
Here becomes there, but how?
Give me the present some more…
You were with me, could see that
It's gone now, that cliff where we sat!

As I put these words on paper
I see each line form and go away
Maybe I'll write a little later…
Yesterday was today like any other day
Every moment was true, yet a dream
Fiction, it might sometimes seem!

Moments of clarity pass with such speed
Faster even then light…
To hold them, I do feel the need
A photo might capture it, but its just sight
Here today – gone tomorrow!
But tomorrow will be today that morrow…

(August 2014)

STAR SONG

Let me journey on amidst this chaos,
Dreams lead me on somewhere
A goal I cannot name, ah! My loss,
A blue sky and green grass, I find even there
The Sun rises and my dreams take a break…
To reveal themselves again, for night, they wait…

Your face in my mind, only reflection
Of memories past, moments lived, now gone
I try and draw you with words, mere diction,
Words fail, even music would, for all you have shown
There he waits with his scythe to sever
I just ask; isn't the forever really for ever?

I turn my face to the Sun and close my eyes
Only stars greet me when I open them again,
Night follows day as sure as that eagle which glides,
Let morn arrive, will witness the Sunrise then
Did I tell you stars are not too bad?
Even in the dark they sing a song that's sad…

(23rd of March 23, 2014)

STILL LOVE YOU

How can you say 'still' in love?
I search below and I search above,
'I still love you', then love it is not,
Once we give our hearts away, love is sought...
Love once found, never does desert,
Time and space might pull you apart
Might take you to a place where you never meet,
Yet, it leaves behind memories sweet.

In memory even, the heart doesn't forget,
Distance between us, yet closer we get!
The three magic words, a softly spoken spell,
I never stopped loving, so I can't say 'still'
Years later, when time has taken her toll,
Isn't it the same for us all?
Memory perhaps is all I have in my heart,
With memory then, I shall silently flirt...

Ah! Let me come out and please show me the way...
You never left even when you went far away!

(Mid August 2013)

TALL TALES OF DISTANT LANDS

Tall tales of distant lands,
Seeing is believing though;
A smile every morning, every day,
Tales of love and of kindness
Meet me before the Sun rises,
Hear all I have to say.
There is one we call the absolute,
Whose life was unparalleled love...

Did such a one ever walk?
Ah! To witness his very sight
Love demands sacrifice in great measure,
Hold on as you would a great treasure
What do I bring you; but early morning chimes
Its time now to wake up
To witness the great dawn of love,
To finally see him and sing our lonely song!

(31 October 2013)

THAT GUST OF WIND

That gust is in recess now
Strong it was, wind nonetheless!
Almost blew away all...
My beliefs
My Understanding
My likes
My dislikes
My Self!
I tasted it first when I saw you
Again, when I felt your words!

A storm unlike any I had seen
Or felt, for that matter
I tried defining it in words:
Love...
Could I call it that?
Passion...
Is this the word I was searching for?
Attraction...
No, these are mere words

That gust was more than all these
It was more than mere words
It happens every time I see you!
Happens now, as it did then...
Thankfully, that gust is in recess now!

(August 2014)

THAT MAN ON THE TREE

During a certain rainy monsoon
A tale took birth, a new tune;
The young man in his tree house
Climbed down the tree to be a part of us
He looked around, and what did he find?
Mankind corrupted, all of the same kind…
Human avarice now surpassed all time
Darker than the dark ages, a sure sign

That man needed a Messiah,
Someone who would show the way without tire!
Disgusted in man's current state,
Our young man took a chalk and wrote on the slate;
"The first reason is Greed,
The second, Intolerance, heed!"
He took upon himself, this task at hand,
His tale soon spread throughout the land!

Before I climb up the tree house in age,
Let us all free those birds we have kept in our cage…

(August 2013)

THE ABYSMAL DEPTHS

The abysmal depths of reasoning
An ocean of facts...
A pool of methods...
Can I not just let reasoning be?
Play my own tune...
Welcome the abstract...
I try to find a reason behind rhythm
Music needs none...
The drums beat heavy...

The answer resides somewhere in history
Pages to turn...
Lives to relive...
Elusive, yet there, beyond reason
To catch a thought...
To let it reside...
Methods are but narrow pathways
Release that thought...
Let being just be...

Without reason,
Without method,
Without domain,
Just let me see!

(JUNE 2014)

THE ARCH OF A RAINBOW

The greater the heights, the worse the fall,
If only contentment had been an ever present friend
Smiling at the world, walking surely, walking tall,
Sadly, even the most cherished dreams come to an end
The arch which every rainbow forms
Is everywhere the same, an unbiased norm…

The heart gladdens that there are some truths
Which are beyond debate and forever there,
Like a filling meal of the choicest fruits.
Even the best are caught in the world's ugly snares,
The only recourse is staying true to oneself,
The answer lies within and within I'll dwelve.

That honey tongued bee will, in the end, sting!
That I chose to trust was after all, my fault,
To innocently believe in everyone is your own downfall,
Now that we see through the façade,
will take it with a pinch of salt
When you are different, its your fault, they say…
They mark you out for gossip, and in secret tears you pay.

I just have one thing to say to you,
You are beautiful because you are different,
You decided not to join the common pack!
Yes, they will laugh at you,
Yes, they will spread lies,
But that's them, and you...
Well, remember that rainbow?
It's different, and beautiful because it is!

(6/4/2014)

THE BURDEN OF DISTRACTION

Thoughts and their willing burden...
Here now, here again and then there
Can I not just hold it, either here or there?
Promises made, but where?

Constant in the belief of this future
Walking through the marsh of that past
A swamp to hold the thoughts...
Finally arriving at this, the future

Arriving at last to accept all
There are but two sides to every coin
Its either here or there,
I just wish I could be in one of them...

And not
Here,
and there!

(May 18, 2014)

THE CENTRIST

Defying gravity, even possible?
   In flight as this tale I tell
A center somewhere in between,
You wouldn't even understand what I mean

A country ravaged by sad sorrow,
   This tale from time I borrow
Let the ruler rule from home,
A government, but from epitome shown!

Let justice flow from the very center,
Let the bird fly searching for its feather,
No power to the states, this kingdom true,
Come, search for the king, this center do!

Now, its just an aftermath
Where was it where the king sat?
Let the center rule even in war
Without center, the states wouldn't go far!

Yes, you could call me a centrist
Call what you will, the way needs this!

(15/07/2014)

THE CHAIR

Sitting in your chair, evening,
People passing by, reckoning!
Your expression joyous when you see
Them passing by, and that tree...
Loneliness comes calling, I know,
Even among friends on the phone...
Your age is a lie
Even to the eye
Numbers they are,
Numbers,
You look Oh! So young, trust,
As you keep looking out
That television noise begins to be sought.
You come back leaving your chair,
Once turning back,
when you breathe the evening air...
Now, it's the news which holds you,
The same cycle everyday and yet, new!

Did I ever tell you,
I love you?

July 2013

THE COLOUR OF LAUGHTER

If feelings could be coloured,
    Would a rainbow form?
If feelings could be heard,
    Would songs find their way home?

That human expression sought by all
    Isn't it true that laughter it is?
On a lucky few we witness its fall,
    We might ponder, but mere emotions these...

A colour then let us give laughter,
    A song we can call out by its name,
Black or maybe white, or any we find better
    A colour carrying along its own fame.

A task I think green would fulfill,
    Nature we witness, and complete our day,
Nature it is, while going uphill,
    A green laughter, red, or a laughter grey...

A colour for laughter, why?
So that we can see it passing by...

(Sept 2013)

HIP HOPPING WITH NATURE

Kindred, I would call you a brother,
A relation nonetheless, unlike any other,
Your presence felt, even in a desert
I chance upon an oasis, you in my heart,
You give me respite, yes you do,
Your dance; when all I see is you…
Nature dancing? Now that's some sight!
Let's beat a rhythm, even in a cold, dark night.

I drew water from a well today,
Thirsty, I guess I'll just let you have your say
The green I see is the green you are
Nature at her best, though I cant see her!
Come now; let's join hands in dance,
Let's beat a rhythm and break the fence
Nature and us, a dance with that lady
Some semblance of a divine comedy…

Hip Hopping away with nature at her greenest
Until finally we earn us some rest!

(5th of January 2014)

THE DIARY

On the table lay yesterday's diary,
All those dates filled up, those moments lived
Pages of mirth, pages of laughter,
Black binding, leather; like lost tears

I came upon you and I could see now
How every today was a brooding pond
Where ripples were those lost tunes,
Which still played in my mind sometimes...

That snatch of a conversation leading to you
That careless belief in a tomorrow,
A tomorrow where the key was a promise...
Where did I go wrong?

When was that exact moment?

I read you again from end to end;
The news is that the rains are foretold
All else is history...
Let me get my umbrella

Let me go back time...

I remember a name there,
I wish I had it written down.

My little lost diary!

(19th of January 2014)

THE EARTH SMILES!

Have you seen the Earth smile?
Every day, you just need a while
I was lucky today; I saw some flowers!
Here, it is the Earth smiling;
Don't know how they do it in Mars…
A touch of the divine in every nook and corner
All we need to do is spare a look, sir!
Flowers everywhere; ah! The Earth smiling true,
A respite from this tedious journey,
they will see us through!
If something so beautiful can be without cause,
Reason enough to gallop through life on that coloured horse!
A rose here, a violet there,
All their beauty, without cause, they share,
I was lucky today, that rose that I saw…
The Earth smiling a divine smile, an unstated law!

(December 2013)

THE GIFT

A simple word taking slow shape,
Arising from the mist as was its fate...
Before the word, man was, but brute,
The Cosmos waiting with her secret loot!
A game, a plan, spanning the Universe,
All of man's philosophy ready to rehearse
Simple joy, and nature's gain it was,
Alike sleeping without worry on that green grass...

As the battle horns marked the beginning of war
Ready to sing the Cosmos's own lore
It had a plan which came to life,
The Universe ready with her secret to come alive...
Witness now, the victor and the vanquished,
But a difference as the plan was released!
The victor let the vanquished raise his head
The Universe waiting with her plan to see where it led

Man was taught in turn to give,
The lights shone upon him, the word was 'forgive'

(21/03/2014)

THE PHILOSOPHER'S STONE

An idea giving birth to a new world,
It was like a sweet dream unfurled.
A dream akin to the bright blue sky,
A dream which reality draws nigh
A shout and a hoorah to welcome it in
I can hear it taking shape even in this din!
The thought we were all waiting for,
A leisurely walk on that peaceful shore…

Now, what was that idea all about?
Science and philosophy, sipping tea, and a talk!
Did you say it first, or, was it I?
Well, it was night and a time when thoughts fly.
This world has forgotten to do what is right,
Letting go when you shouldn't let it out of sight,
Then flew in a fancy white dove,
Ah! Remembered the idea, it was simply called 'love'!

(8th of March 2013)

THE REASON BEHIND

The reason; the reason behind,
Even before we see, we look for
Every known phenomena
And some unknown...
Does every effect have a cause?
Does everything known
Have to have a reason behind?

I say; stars are just as wonderful
Unknown...
Flowers smell as sweet
Without cause...
Love is even more beautiful
Without the 'why'...
Dreams still leave a smile
Without interpretation...

Love, now love needs no introduction,
Every human heart has felt
Its magnificence in some measure,
Gladly we fall into its throes,
Gladly...
Without reason...
Without cause...

Now that's something to search for,
A reason to be...

(17TH of Nov 2013)

THE RIVER (Brahmaputra)

Every morn, as I set out from home,
Your picture arising from the mist; shown.
I noticed your turbulence today,
Did someone anger you? Have your say...
Mostly calm, mostly benign
I look at you, as I would at a sign!
You show me, in that moment I cross,
All in life, that I have come across...
The past, the present and the future,
You possess all, ah! It's in your nature
I leave you behind, O mighty wonder!
Hoping to come back to witness your splendor...

The day proceeds...
Approaches an end...

I come back again after work is done
The road, and you there, after the turn!
A little spent but you awaken me
Your waters dark, aye; in you, me, I see!
Tomorrow is another day, I'll meet you again,
That's the truth, I concur in words plain...

(20th of February 2014)

THE SELF AND TIME

Up towards a distant dream aglow
With thoughts on the nature of time,
Distant, yet within reach...
Not yet! Not yet!
Wait...
Waiting: an essence of time
Being: an essence of self
Love?
Time now to bring it all together
Time now to usher in the tides
A calm ocean, ripples of joy
Fight with uncalled for sorrow
Yet a dream...
Aglow!
I look inside and suddenly realize
That all these years have passed
In seconds
Its all in the now
For now is eternity
Let me search further
Let me hold time in my hands
I cant, I fail,
For time is like the sand
Slips through my fingers
Into hard land!

(10th of Nov, 2013)

THE TWIN PATHS

He walked on the road life laid out before him,
Looked back and saw it had all been a dream
Everyone he had ever met, now in guise,
Some still there, some gone, all a disguise
Even tears refused to do his bidding,
Coming unannounced, sometimes not at all, a constant ring!

He let the game unravel before him,
To live every moment, hard though it may seem
The first question never met its answer,
Yes, it was she; could he ever forget her?
The questions that followed were a different story,
All of them somehow had tinges of history.

Now he saw two paths laid out,
To grasp their meaning, with himself bout!
The first led away from it all, the world and her ways,
The second embracing the world, her nights and her days,
The choice not easy, though his alone,
A song all his, his path, his tone!

(13th of April 2014)

THIS AND THAT, HERE AND THERE

Droplets upon the windowpane
Thoughts too...forming themselves,
Night now, wade with great care
Silence...except for that empty glance
Tell me now
Is it the same everywhere?
Guest of your own creation
Thoughts and their willing burden
Feel me and say that it
matters not...
Freedom is all I got...
All I want...
All I have!

(June 2014)

TOMORROW

Soaring, like a bird in flight,
Almost touching that untamed blue,
Illusion lasts, but for seconds
Back again to that solitary nest,
Tomorrow is another flight,
Tomorrow is another dream
Tomorrow is…
Thankful it is…

Is freedom an ideal worth fighting for?
Is blue ever reflected in our hearts?
If love had a colour, it would be blue
If freedom had one…
Well, white is as good as any,
Tomorrow is…
Thankful it is…

(22nd May 2014)

'TWAS LOVE

Does it mean we talk no more?
I erred but my heart was true,
Pain the release, that bond with you
Even now, when I have lost the key to that door
I look out, see the clouds above,
Hope their promise finds expression in rain
All I am left with is this numbing pain!

Sometimes I say your name out loud
just so I can hear it said out,
I close my eyes and catch a glimpse of you,
So Far away, all I see is the colour blue
Ah! Love is such a common word,
It would take more to express my heart…
I smile now only when I have my eyes closed!

(September 7, 2014)

TWICE

Twice, he heard the bell ring,
Before he would have let it go
Now he knew it was time to wake up
Now he knew twice was
One too many...

Puddles on his way, he was used to,
Roadblocks many created at whim
By forces beyond his meager span
Beyond his knowledge, now he needed
Life without hinder...

Courage, he hoped, would come to him
At his beckoning, a silent will,
Courage to face what was brought on
By the ringing bells, by providence,
By absolute chance...

He awoke at last to his destiny
Brought on by that gambling chance
He awoke to see himself free
In the mirror placed before him
Twice, was what it took...

(2nd of Nov 2013)

UNCONDITIONAL LOVE

All we really need is one person,
Who would believe even through adversity,
Who would peg even his own dreams to yours
Who will say, I know you will succeed,
Even when you don't…

One who would smile at your joy,
Cry at your tears,
Wink at your jokes,
'Unconditional love' sounds like two dreamy words…
But when we have found it, we are home!

Seriously though, is it even possible?
Don't we all live on, believing in it?
Yes…we do!
Yes…we do!
That's what keeps us human,

Those two dreamy words
Are all there is to life,
All one could ever want
Unconditional love…

(8th of April 2014)

UNDERSTANDING YOU

Understanding you is often so hard
Mankind, I say this, though we've journeyed far!
A ritualistic sacrifice made on an alter of gold,
It would require more than just blood, require letters bold
I saw your tears and thought you were sad,
I tried to make you smile but tears were all you had
Let me play the clown now,
I just wish to see you smile and how!

Your happiness intact in a place secret,
You never show it, do you, but do you regret?
We could have had so many happy moments
Even imagining it makes me go tense!
But I want to, yes, I want to understand,
See through the veil and play my winning hand
Ah! Out with it now! Let me in on...
That secret; so that happiness can be drawn!

Understanding you is often so hard...

(1st of Jan 2014)

WALKING ALONE

Walking alone is easy,
Almost...
Until that moment when you wish
That you actually had someone,
Anyone...
Who could speak your heart's tongue
Who could converse without needing words!
In silence...
Man is made tough, or is he?
Nature dictates the rhythm and the dance,
Naïve...
Enough to believe he can go on
In the walk of life on his very own,
Reality...
Even when he sings alone,
You could catch that woman in his song,
Incomplete...
Until you actually meet her,
Know she is the one,
Woman...
Walking alone is easy,
Almost...

(24th of April 2014)

WHO TOIL WITHOUT REST

Her feet tiring, her brow sweaty,
Up at the crack of dawn...
Even before light, on her journey,
First, it's the grass she mows, on that lawn!
Then she's there for the road,
Without complain, she picks up her daily load...

Yet a smile keeps playing on her face!

Yes, she is old now, yes, tiring.
Giving up though, is just not her lot,
She walks into town, swaggering,
Her wrinkles reflecting the battles she's fought.
Old, yet young! Asking for more...
Taking life, like the sea walking to shore!

Yet a smile keeps playing on her face!

Her journey reminiscent of the best,
A respite for all who toil without rest!

(15th of December 15, 2013)

WISE IS THE MAN WHO KNOWS

Wise is the man who knows;
Joyous, the ones who listen,
That sad, sure, drumbeat
A voice beyond the throes
Of crazy silence,
Of meaning,
Of laughter,
Of tears...
Ah! To hear him speak

Tales that touch us true,
Rendering our hearts blue

A domain beyond the unknown
Beyond being,
Beyond words,
Beyond joy,
Beyond suffering...

Let us gather and hear
Him speaking those magic words
Telling us how to be
Is there such a one?

Search, as we would,

Our essence,

Our existence,

Our love,

Our pain...

We have names we call him by,

Yet, we search on...

For, wise is the man who knows.

(16th of Oct, 2013)